# BELIEF BOUND MIND

## My Journey from a wheelchair to living LIFE on my own terms

AARON TIMMS

Copyright © 2019 Aaron Timms.

All rights reserved. No part of this book may be used or reproduced by any means, graphic, electronic, or mechanical, including photocopying, recording, taping or by any information storage retrieval system without the written permission of the author except in the case of brief quotations embodied in critical articles and reviews.

This book is a work of non-fiction. Unless otherwise noted, the author and the publisher make no explicit guarantees as to the accuracy of the information contained in this book and in some cases, names of people and places have been altered to protect their privacy.

Balboa Press books may be ordered through booksellers or by contacting:

Balboa Press
A Division of Hay House
1663 Liberty Drive
Bloomington, IN 47403
www.balboapress.com
1 (877) 407-4847

Because of the dynamic nature of the Internet, any web addresses or links contained in this book may have changed since publication and may no longer be valid. The views expressed in this work are solely those of the author and do not necessarily reflect the views of the publisher, and the publisher hereby disclaims any responsibility for them.

The author of this book does not dispense medical advice or prescribe the use of any technique as a form of treatment for physical, emotional, or medical problems without the advice of a physician, either directly or indirectly. The intent of the author is only to offer information of a general nature to help you in your quest for emotional and spiritual well-being. In the event you use any of the information in this book for yourself, which is your constitutional right, the author and the publisher assume no responsibility for your actions.

Any people depicted in stock imagery provided by Getty Images are models,
and such images are being used for illustrative purposes only.
Certain stock imagery © Getty Images.

Print information available on the last page.

ISBN: 978-1-9822-3307-5 (sc)
ISBN: 978-1-9822-3308-2 (hc)
ISBN: 978-1-9822-3309-9 (e)

Library of Congress Control Number: 2019912227

Balboa Press rev. date: 08/14/2019

Knowledge is power, but the key to knowledge is awareness.

—*Aaron Timms*

As you will see below, I have decided to include one of the poems in my book that I wrote while I was in Romford Hospital, in intensive care. This is a very personal and a difficult decision for me to make. I have chosen to include this because I am asking you to be brave throughout the book. As we look in the mirror together, if I expect you to be brave, I must show bravery to you in the first instance.

I also believe that for you to really have belief in my teachings, you need to understand or relate to the dark place that I really came from. My story is as real as it gets, and I feel strongly that you should hear it all.

**Rest in Peace, Soulmates**

Donna you were the best thing in my life, without your love I just can't
cope. One day, you were to be my wife, but for you, I'll live in hope.
Forever you'll both live on in my heart. I love you so much
and Oli too. Deep, deep down inside, I promise we'll never
be apart. I promise, baby girl—me, Oli, and you.
I hope you look down on me and help me through. Both
guide me like a star. I need you to. Maybe one day, we can
meet again. Until that day, I long for you, my friend.
You were my lover, friend, and soulmate. At least I found you in life—
this makes me feel great. You're in a better place than me. I hope you're
with Oli and pain-free. Right now, with you is where I'd rather be.

I love you both—rest in peace.
x x From me x x

# ACKNOWLEDGEMENTS

First of all, I would like to thank my wonderful wife, Amy Timms, for her continued support. She gives me constant love, kindness, and friendship, which has enabled me to focus on making this book the best it can be.

There have been many teachers along my journey and many wonderful people whom I owe deeply, but here are just a few I must thank personally:

I would like to say a huge thank you to my stepmother, Cathy Timms. She gave me the tools and knowledge I needed to start this wonderful journey.

Possibly my biggest inspiration is Dr Joe Dispenza. His approach to teaching the power of the mind in such a scientific and spiritual way is truly inspiring.

Last but not least, I owe the biggest thank you to my parents, Jane Tucker and Stephen Timms. They both taught me life lessons no money in the world could buy. For that, I will be eternally grateful.

Dad, thank you for being my hero. Thank you for being the rock that I needed in my toughest times and guiding through life without fear. Thank you for holding my hand and leading me over all the mountains that were put in my way.

Mum, thank you for making me realise my own value and for making me feel like no dream was too big. You are the reason I believe in myself so much. Thank you for being you and teaching me my values, which define me.

# 1

# THE POWER OF YOUR MIND

Unbelievable! To this day, I still have to pinch myself when I look in the mirror. I see this powerful, healthy man who leads, teaches, and instils belief in people. I have to digest the fact that this is *really* me.

When you hear my story, you will have real-life proof of the power of the mind. Why am I so confident? Because I went from being a paralyzed man to one who could stand tall and walk again, much to the initial disbelief of the medical community. Against all odds, I harnessed the power of my mind to achieve a nearly unthinkable goal.

I was in a serious traffic accident in which I was left paralyzed, and I saw two loved ones, my best friend and my girlfriend, die before my very eyes. I am now healed in every sense of the word. I am truly happy and healthy, and the wealth I have created is just a by-product of understanding the power of my mind.

You may be wondering how on earth I got through this! The answer is actually simple—believe it or not, it requires complete control and understanding of your mind. This will become simple to do and understand as you learn practical ways to do this in my book.

You will have an opportunity to achieve anything and everything you desire. Yes, everything! You will discover the power of the mind to such an extent that you can heal yourself of illness and injury, find inner peace, achieve balance, and even create wealth!

This may seem extreme to read so early in the book, but believe me—I have a discovered something so powerful and so pure that it's simply life-changing. The wonderful news is that you already have the necessary tool to achieve anything you want—it's the power of your mind.

*Life is wonderful.* No matter where you are, what your profession is, what your problems are, whether you are young or old, and how serious your injuries may be, this book will help you see yourself and your life in a new light. The feeling of contentment and true happiness that I now feel is overwhelming when I look back at the traumas of the last decade.

In this book, you will hear the harrowing but inspiring story about my life-changing accident, which has brought me to this place of absolute happiness. Absolute happiness comes from within us and is a feeling that is abundant and there for *all* to experience.

People often say to me, "How can I achieve absolute happiness?" The truth is that contentment and true happiness are found differently in each and every one of us. There is no correct or incorrect way. This book will offer wonderful techniques and knowledge for you to manifest in abundance, in all areas of your life, as you find your own path.

Not that long ago, I was a man who was seriously injured, paralyzed, broke, and depressed. Yet, because I harnessed the power of my mind, I now have an incredible story to share with you. You'll learn how I came to be in a position of power, happiness, and wealth in all areas of my life.

My definition of wealth is *abundance* in all areas of my life. For me, an abundance of time, happy relationships, good health in body and mind, and money make me wealthy.

If you're thinking, "Why should I believe this author? Who is he?" It's simple. I am living proof of the power of the mind. When this journey started, I was in intensive care, paralyzed and grieving for the loss of two dear people; I was broken. Now, I am 100 per cent healthy, content, happy, and wealthy!

Are you ready to change your life? Do you want to create health, wealth, and contentment? Read on as I guide you on your journey, helping you balance your spiritual self, your law of attraction, your deliberate practice, and your ability to take action today.

This book will teach you how to take control of your own life and your own destiny! While you read my story, I invite you to be open, to believe, and be inspired.

## Stop! Take a Moment!

Before you read this book, please ask yourself out loud, "What would make me feel content?"

____________________________________________

____________________________________________

"What is my idea of absolute happiness?"

____________________________________________

____________________________________________

Do your decisions take you directly towards your idea of happiness?

____________________________________________

____________________________________________

Do you want to be wealthy? If so, why? If not, why not?

____________________________________________

____________________________________________

Leave all limitations behind you and open your mind to the limitless opportunities that are there for you each and every day. Do not be afraid to be honest! Being honest with yourself is brave—be brave!

I live life on my own terms.

—*Aaron Timms*

# 2

## TRIUMPH OVER TRAUMA

The day I looked death straight in the eyes was the day that changed the course of my life forever. Although I suffered tremendous losses, I was also *gifted* with a different perspective, a new way of thinking, and a spiritual understanding. The reason I am standing here today completely healed and writing this book is that I harnessed the power of my mind and believed that there was more in store for me.

I could have easily survived the physical trauma only to suffer *mental anguish* for the rest of my life. Fortunately, that was not an option for me, and I will share with you what I learned and how I did it.

The date was Monday, 22 September 2008. I was 21 years old, and it was my friend's twenty-fourth birthday. My best friend, my girlfriend, and I celebrated his birthday with a meal. We all enjoyed a wonderful evening, yet there was no way to predict what would happen next.

It was time to drive home in my girlfriend's small car. It only had two doors, which required climbing over the seats to get to the back. Driving to the restaurant, I was in the front seat on account of the cast on my broken ankle from a football injury. On the way home, I did something different.

Knowing now that *this decision is what saved my life* still overwhelms me with many different emotions.

I was waiting by the car for my friend to climb into the rear seat first, but he was taking his time. Because the wind was freezing and I was uncomfortable, I decided to make the extremely awkward climb onto the rear seat.

From this point onward, my memories are chequered yet vivid and precise. *This journey would be the last for us all together.* I do not remember the main part of the journey, but I do remember very clearly the few seconds before, which strangely felt like hours at the time of the event.

The tires lost their grip, and our car lost control, sending us straight for the curb. We flipped upside-down before hitting a lamppost while in midair. The noises were loud and intense; there were desperate screams and the sound of metal tearing and glass shattering. It was simply terrifying.

Bang! Immediately following was such a silence that I realized I was amongst death. I did not know at the time who was dead, but I could sense a dead energy. Although I had never been close to death before, somehow my subconscious mind understood this.

For thirty minutes, I hung upside down with lifeless legs, screaming uncontrollably out of fear and pain. Admittedly, death was the more appealing option at the time.

Then there was commotion—I heard metal being forced and torn and saw faces and bright lights. I was so frightened. The firefighters cut me out of the vehicle, and the medics carefully removed me so that I could be rushed to the local A & E for possible head injuries and a broken spine.

*What was happening to me? Where were the others?* So many traumatic thoughts were rushing through my head that I hadn't even considered how serious my injuries could be. I was frantic and panicking, and the hospital staff had to calm me down with strong medication.

When my mother arrived, the relief I felt was immense, but it was quickly clouded by the overwhelming feeling of fear when I saw the look on her face. I knew she was trying to hide it as best she could, but she was clearly terrified. Although my mother knew the terrible news about the others—that they had both been killed upon impact—she was incredibly strong in waiting for the right time to deliver the news, no matter how hard I begged.

After a CT scan, the doctor officially delivered the news to me about my friend and girlfriend. I couldn't stop the desperate and incredibly painful emotion leaving my body in the form of a childlike howling/screaming sound. It tore through me like a blunt knife, and the rage and anger were so strong.

"Why?" I kept asking. It felt so unfair. I had never felt such pain. I felt as if I were in a nightmare and I couldn't wake up. I thought my life was over, and I didn't even care. Having felt that definite still energy of death in the car, deep down, I had already known, but the doctor removed all hope that one of them had survived.

My mother held me tightly as we both cried uncontrollably. As if being paralyzed wasn't enough, I was now facing grief and survivor's guilt on an intense level!

When my father appeared, I was lying down, strapped to the stretcher, staring at the ceiling lights, almost in a trancelike state. It was the oddest feeling to see his face; he was so calm on the outside, and his energy was strong and powerful. I felt like a child who needed reassurance, and I felt this in abundance. I knew how distraught he was, but he remained calm and incredibly composed, which was exactly what I needed.

What happened next was quite incredible!

I saw a man at the end of my bed, a white silhouette, and he spoke to me. I couldn't hear exactly what was said as my body was in shock, but I know he was speaking directly to me.

"What did he say, Dad?" I shouted. "What did he say?"

"There is nobody there, mate. Calm down," my father said.

"Don't lie to me, Dad! What did the doctor say?" I asked.

Again, he said, "I promise, mate. Nobody is there."

This went on because I knew what I saw, and I was convinced my father was lying to protect me. I knew that I saw *somebody*. There was no doubt in my mind at all. The image is still clear in my mind to this day and probably always will be.

At the time, I thought my vision was impaired due to shock and medication, but I now know this was the energy of my friend passing from life to death. He was moving on and came to say goodbye for the last time. It may be hard for you, the reader, to comprehend what I am describing, but once you have seen and experienced this for yourself, it is easy to accept and understand.

Because my injuries were too serious, I was airlifted from the Colchester General Hospital to Romford Hospital to see a specialist in the neurological unit.

For the following six days, I waited for a prognosis and news about my surgery and recovery. I drifted in and out of consciousness, desperately trying to make some sense of the situation but failing every time.

The day of my operation finally arrived. There was no room for error, as my spinal cord was dislocated and broken, as well as losing spinal fluid. Any incorrect decisions or movements meant the cord would be severed completely.

The operation took a total of eight hours and was considered a success. The general anaesthetic provided full pain relief and unbroken rest for the first time since the accident. The operation gave my mind a much-needed rest.

As I came around, I was instantly searching for a sense of relief, for somebody to say, "It's OK. The nightmare is over," but that was far from reality.

I had no feeling, function, or control of my body at all from the waist down. The realisation that I was disabled was intense and odd. Strangely, this disability was not terrifying at this point, because I think my subconscious mind went into denial as a built-in coping mechanism. It is also possible that I was so depressed, my conscious mind did not care enough to be terrified.

At this point, I had survived a traumatic car accident and received a successful surgery. What happened next was incredible, and it was all because my father wisely withheld information from me.

After my operation, the consultants told him that due to the damage my spinal cord and central nervous system had sustained, *I would never walk again*. At best, I might have some feeling and slight movement, but I wouldn't ever be able to hold up my own body weight.

My father begged them not to tell my mother or me because neither of us was ready to hear this. As I was over eighteen, this went against protocol, but my dad argued that I had lost two people whom I loved dearly, and it wasn't the right time.

They eventually agreed to let my father tell us both when he felt the time was right.

My mother and I both believed that I was being transferred to Stoke Mandeville to *learn to walk again*, but the truth was that I was being transferred to prepare me for life in a wheelchair.

To this day, I know that this act of strength and bravery by my father is *the reason I am walking and fully recovered.*

Much later, and well after the fact, I found out that while I was having my operation, my dad sat in the car praying. Cathy (my stepmother) sat down beside him and said that she could visualize an image of me with a blonde wife and a baby. (Read on to find out how *incredibly accurate* this vision would be!) After hearing her words, Dad believed without a doubt that despite all the difficulties, *I would walk again.*

The aim of writing this and sharing my story of the path to enlightenment and happiness is to show that not everyone has to go through what I did. From my experience, you can learn these lessons without having to have experienced this yourself.

As you will discover throughout this book, to unlock the true power of your mind, you need to *believe 100 per cent.* Without a doubt, my father's decision instilled that belief in my mind. He believed, and importantly, I truly believed. And that is just the beginning of my seemingly mysterious and miraculous journey.

## Stop, Take a Moment!

Take a moment to try and imagine being a young, fit, and healthy 21-year-old man, loving life, enjoying sports and a great social life. In the blink of an eye, you are put into a dark world of grief and disability. Can you imagine? It's no wonder that I did not know how to feel at the time. I knew what I felt in the car—the dead energy—but I also knew that the silhouette I saw in A & E was a tremendous gift.

What heartaches, pain, tragedy, and trauma are you carrying with you? Have you come to peace with them? What have you learned from them? Were you able to let them go, or did you let them fuel you?

I healed myself when I had 0 per cent chance.

*—Aaron Timms*

# 3

# BUILDING BELIEF

If I had submitted to the idea that I would never walk again, I guarantee that I would be in a wheelchair right now. If I had abandoned all hope and not believed that I had the power to overcome any obstacle, I would not be where or who I am today. I wouldn't be writing this book, and I wouldn't be helping countless people live their best life.

*But I did believe.*

My spinal injuries were so severe that doctors described them as "life-changing injuries with no chance of ever walking again". Fortunately, before I heard this news, I had committed to the belief that I would get the magical physio I needed to walk again. I diligently researched the miraculous recoveries from patients at Stoke Mandeville and anxiously awaited my transfer.

Brace yourself for a powerful lesson in building belief.

I was suffering, in pain, and grieving, experiencing flashbacks, nightmares, rage, and survivor's guilt. I didn't have enough headspace to keep looking back while working on recovery and rehabilitation. I felt as if I didn't deserve to even be alive, let alone focus on myself.

Even with good upper-body strength, I couldn't sit up in bed let alone face the physical strain and anguish of transferring to and sitting in a wheelchair.

A concerned nurse said to me, "This may seem selfish, but it is very important that your legs are your best friends right now." My initial thought was that this was a ridiculous thing to say, but on reflection, those were very wise words. What she was saying to me was that I could not change the outcome for the others involved, and I needed to have the strength and focus on my legs and rehabilitation.

I remember staring at my feet, trying to come to terms with the reality of my injuries, but all I could see were a stranger's feet. This is a feeling I cannot put into words.

My subconscious mind was desperately trying to find cognitive ways to cope, so I reached out to the chaplain at Romford Hospital. I asked for his blessing to put my grief on hold temporarily so I could put all my energy into conquering my injuries.

I knew I could not do both at the same time.

When I was finally able to sit up and transfer into a wheelchair, it was an immense victory. I used all my strength and grit and fed off the encouragement of my family and the hospital staff.

After spending weeks in bed, being in the wheelchair was exciting but also very daunting. I felt weak and vulnerable. I remember being afraid to be pushed over a small lip in the carpet on the floor—it sounds very extreme now, but that level of fear within me was very real at the time, I can assure you.

My family and friends were wonderfully supportive and gave me strength, helping me to battle against the fear. But I could see they were all struggling as well. This was tough for me to watch.

After three weeks at Romford, it was difficult to say goodbye to the nurses, as they had been by my side in my darkest hour. They not only were excellent at their profession but also were wonderful people. The nurses had gone far above the call of duty for me. They had been precise about my physical care, tended to my erratic emotional outbursts, and held my hand through the initial stages of grieving with amazing calmness and wisdom.

The journey to my rehabilitation is one of hope and belief. I truly believed I was on my way to a special place where miracles happened, Stoke Mandeville, and this was my chance, my time!

Ironically, looking back, I now know that due to my belief and mindset this was the exact truth, the only difference being that miracle *was simply a true state of mind*, nothing more.

I arrived at Stoke Mandeville and began with a challenging initial assessment of several unsuccessful blood draws—it was certainly not how I pictured things would go. I was soon ready to meet my main consultant at Stoke Mandeville, "Mr Newton". He was a tall, well-dressed, gentle-looking man. He had a refreshing energy and seemed positive, much more like the doctors I had been imagining while at Romford Hospital. After he explained, with a calm demeanour, that I would be under his care throughout my stay at Stoke Mandeville, he began pricking me with a needle to determine where I had still had feeling. As was to be expected, I felt nothing from the waist down.

When Mr Newton left the room, seemingly in high spirits, he turned and said to us, "Well, at least he will make a great paraplegic." *What?* This comment hit my family and me like a steam train head-on.

*I was here to learn to walk, not to make a good paraplegic.* I was going to prove Mr Newton wrong. Wait and see.

The thought of living my life in a wheelchair was not an option to me. Ironically, the fear of that situation provided all the motivation anybody could ever need. Looking back now, I was actually blessed to be in this mindset.

One of the most difficult things to achieve when striving towards huge goals is to keep up one's motivation, which came naturally to me. Motivation is vital and is one of the main tools a person can use to focus and create the energy required to act.

My belief was vital for numerous reasons. The power of your mind is the *most powerful force in the universe* but only when it is being used to its full potential. I was prepared to do whatever it took in order to stand on my own two feet again.

## Stop, Take a Moment!

Take this opportunity to ask yourself what you believe in. Do you believe that no matter what has happened to you, no matter the hardship or trauma, there is more in store? That you are capable of greatness or a higher purpose? That everything happens for a reason? Now, think of a time when your belief helped you through a traumatic, painful, or difficult situation. What is limiting you from believing in yourself right now?

______________________________________________

______________________________________________

______________________________________________

______________________________________________

______________________________________________

______________________________________________

> I live life by choice, not by chance.
>
> —*Aaron Timms*

# 4

# THE POWER OF ENERGY

Take a moment to imagine having limitless power to achieve whatever you would like to achieve! Close your eyes and imagine your mind harnessing all the energy in the universe to achieve a specific goal. You are well on your way.

*The power of energy needs to be made clear.* Everything is energy—our thoughts and our movements are energy, and a burst of energy, a fit of rage, sparked the catalyst for how I regained the ability to walk again. This was all thanks to energy.

In this chapter, I'd like to teach you how to harness your energy, both positive and negative, so that you can achieve your goals.

Although others at Stoke Mandeville were accepting of their fate, I *refused.* I was so fed up with being in bed and feeling sorry for myself that I demanded to see a physio. I convinced myself that I had installed the belief, possessed the motivation, and could generate the energy required to walk again.

All I could think about was walking, running even. I would lay in bed for hours and hours, trying to move my legs and intensely imagining playing football again. The real key to this powerful exercise is creating a new reality in this moment. Making the experience feel very real. I would close my eyes and feel I was playing football. I would feel the grass under my feet and that magic cold sponge one of the parents would always use to cure any injury!

The feeling you create in your mind is what will create potential energy. You don't need to concern yourself with how this works. Just believe that it does.

When I was trying to get my head around this, it was important not to get too mixed up in the science of it. The fact is I have very little knowledge of any science. So what? I know how to use it. Do I try to understand what electricity is every time I use it? No, because it does not matter—it works.

It was also very important for me to focus on *my* journey and *my* body; it is easy to compare yourself to others who have travelled the journey you are now traveling. They may have failed for their own reasons, but this does not mean you will. If you feel the need to follow somebody before you, like I did, choose a person that *succeeded.*

I chose to follow Bruce Lee. A true story that many people do not know is that before he became very famous, he broke his back just like I did, and he healed himself using the power of his mind. I highly recommend you watch the film *Dragon*, a story of his life, and really look at how he successfully controlled his own mind.

I had done my research, and I was ready to fight against the world and revved up to work with my physio. At our first appointment, the physio said, "Stop it right there. Your legs won't work, and I am *not* going to work with your legs. I need to train you to use a wheelchair to help you learn how to get out of bed by yourself and how to transfer to a car. Respectfully, if anything happens with your legs, we'll look at it then, but for now, let's get you mobile in the wheelchair."

These words angered me to my core, and the resulting ball of rage was so powerful that I lost it then and there. I started throwing things in the hospital room, and although I couldn't really move, my arms were going. My stepfather came into the room and gripped me tightly until I was calm.

I didn't realize what I'd done at the time, because my injury was fresh. But because I still had vivid memories of running and walking and of being physically strong, I pictured myself running in anger. I created so much powerful energy from this reaction of the physio that I demanded,

"How dare you tell me you won't help me work on my legs?" I took this forceful negative energy and visualized my legs running.

Brace yourself because this is special. Against all the odds, especially so early on, I had muscle twitches in my thighs! This was even before any swelling had gone down, and no logical explanation could be applied as to why this was happening.

What I had done, without quite realizing at the time, was create so much energy that *I created new connections in my brain*, which then fired down my spinal cord. According to my doctor, because I'd lost spinal fluid and scar tissue was forming, messages like these could no longer go through my body properly, because the electronic connections had no path through.

The power of energy proved that theory to be incorrect.

I immediately called the doctor to tell him what had happened and said, "Look! I've got twitches in my legs!" I was told that they were probably spasms known as "impulsive muscle twitches", but I knew that wasn't right and found that response very frustrating.

I obviously didn't understand about potential and kinetic energy and making connections in my brain at the time. But what I knew was that I had to harness that frustration into hard work. Clearly, I didn't have to understand the how or the why for this to work.

To me, this is obvious: *I had such an intense energy and focus in my mind* at one single moment in time that this energy was directed into my legs. My mind had forced this energy down through my spinal cord, complete with scar tissue, through my nervous system and into the muscles in my legs.

The power of manifestation had taken place within me, and this was amazing.

Let's talk about energy for a moment. Imagine that I've got this band on my wrist, and as I'm pulling that band, I'm creating potential energy. As I release, it is quickly converted to kinetic energy. Potential is an energy that's *stored* and kinetic is the energy of *motion*.

Think of how energy is transmitted. Imagine that I'm sitting here, very calm, talking to you, relaxed and barely moving. Suddenly, someone whispers into my ear a piece of information that outrages me. Perhaps it's that my wife has crashed my brand-new car. Even if it isn't true, if I believe it, it will create a reaction. I start waving my fist, my face gets hot, and my heart starts pounding. In my mind, I have created such a scenario that I can no longer sit still and store the energy.

If you can harness this energy in a positive way, it's amazing. Have you ever gotten so angry that you started cleaning, lifting weights, or going for a run? You took negative energy and harnessed it towards something productive.

I have read a wonderful book called *The Secret to Success,* by Eric Thomas. Even with limited scientific knowledge, he was able to explain energy in a way that I think you may relate to. You have the power at any time to create as much potential energy with your mind, using your thoughts, as you desire. It is your choice and responsibility. An incredibly powerful quote from Eric Thomas reads, "Desire and imagination can be classified as potential energy, desire and imagination can be stored in the mind of the individual, but when stretched, both have the power to position a person."

This is what happened when I channelled the potential energy I created with my mind through my legs, which made my muscles twitch. The energy was so intensely powerful and created only a small twitch, which highlights both the severity of my injury and the energy and focus required to heal.

I must be completely honest with you—at the time this happened, I did not understand this fully or how I had done it, but I knew I had. Mr Newton disagreed with this at the time, and he asked my father to be careful of the fact that these might be impulsive nervous twitches. Although I understand why Mr Newton was fearful of letting me build my hopes, I also have a very strong opinion that he should not have disagreed.

As you will learn throughout this book, hope and belief is the key to unlocking the true power of the mind, and Mr Newton could have jeopardized this had I listened to him. I would like to point out the fact that Mr Newton was a wonderful and intelligent man. He was a priest in his previous career and is now a spinal injury specialist at the highest level, but he is human, and it is possible for him to be wrong. Remember this next time you disagree with an expert in one's profession, particularly in the health profession. It's *your* body and your mind, so it is *your* choice.

## Stop, Take a Moment!

When you understand the power of energy, you realize how vital it can be in achieving your goals. Take a minute to close your eyes and visualize a situation that will bring out energy or emotion. Perhaps it was a sports victory, a milestone, or an incident in a relationship. Relive it. It doesn't matter if it is good or bad. Understand the power of thought and understand the power of energy. Write down this event and then record how you reacted versus how you wanted to react.

Rather than reacting instinctively in the future, gather your thoughts, be aware, and do the opposite of what your instincts tell you to do. You're training your mind for future situations. I'm at a point now where I'm so aware, I know that if something makes me angry now, it can almost be fun, because I know I'll have so much energy to get jobs done that I didn't want to do. At this moment, if you feel fired up, I encourage you to apply that energy, right now, towards something productive.

> Nobody can change or heal until they change their energy.
>
> —*Aaron Timms*

# 5

# MIND-BODY CONNECTION

Are you aware that you can create new connections in your brain that can be sent through your body to heal? I wanted to walk as much as I wanted to breathe! I still do! When you want to achieve something that much, you *will* achieve it.

When we wake up in the morning, we have a pre-programmed set of thoughts and actions. Remember—there's always an exception to the rule, but generally speaking, we are creatures of subconscious habit.

For a lot of people, it might be that we wake up, pick up our phone and check social media, go to use the toilet, and then shower. In that process, upon first waking, the mind has thought, "I'm going to check social media," so your body follows, picks up the phone and checks it, and so on.

I'm going to share a personal story and then give an overview of the mind—how it works and how it is inextricably linked to our body.

One of the rehabilitation team members at Stoke Mandeville booked me onto a lecture by a previous patient who was living life in a wheelchair. I refused to attend. In my opinion, respectfully, this was a waste of time. After all, I was not going to be in a wheelchair for the rest of my life, and I felt very strongly about this decision.

Many people who cared for me deeply were afraid that I was in denial at this point, but I was not willing to accept my fate at all. *This is crucial. Take control of your own destiny. It is your choice and nobody else's.*

The same day, Mr Newton paid me a surprise visit. I thought I was going to be in trouble for refusing the lecture, but this was not at all the case. He came to congratulate me on having such strong will power and said that he understood my point of view. What he said next was truly astonishing.

"Aaron, with the movement you have achieved in your legs, now there is *no reason* you will not walk again!" The sense of achievement I experienced at that moment made me feel as if I had just started walking again! I had instilled belief into the most sceptical people of all. My leg movements were still very weak and small and barely beyond twitches at this point, but I believe the medical staff were witnessing the *healing that my mind was creating*. They could not deny what they were seeing!

The true belief that I was going to overcome all odds and walk again had now been instilled into the majority, not the minority! This is a huge milestone for several reasons; one, in particular, is that the people who surround you can have a huge influence on your train of thoughts.

Put simply, if you are surrounded by happy, positive people, you are far more likely to be happy and positive. If you are surrounded by successful people, you are far more likely to be successful. Now that I was surrounded by people with the same beliefs that I had, I could use far less energy battling those negative views and far more energy focussing on achieving my goals.

Not once did the thought of giving up or accepting the wheelchair enter my head. I spent extended periods meditating and imagining walking again, and I visualized walking so much that my legs would physically ache. Now, what does that tell you? *The mind was actually working those muscles.* They might not have been moving enough to see, but the muscle fibres were twitching so much they were aching!

The results were astonishing, and I could barely believe my eyes when I saw what I was capable of doing when I got back in the gym. My mother and stepfather were visiting, and we decided to go to the gym so I could show them the electric-powered exercise bikes. The bikes measure how much input your legs are having so you can measure any improvement in strength. I couldn't resist the chance to get on and have a go, an opportunity not to be missed. The difference was incredible! My legs were 300 per cent stronger than before. I was still very weak, of course. Previously, all my strength had amounted to tiny muscle twitches that were barely visible to the naked eye.

The amount of improvement I experienced just by using the power of my mind is the point here. I now had proof that I could send signals from my brain, through my nervous system, and into my muscles just by using my imagination. Also, I had proof that this energy was stimulating the damaged nerves to heal my spinal cord and was waking up my muscles.

The overwhelming feeling of true belief I felt was incredible, and my determination was becoming difficult to hold back. I knew I was going to walk, and I had just proved this to myself—and, in my view, to all the doubters as well.

Again, I wish to emphasise the fact that true belief is what fuels the full potential of your mind. You must have true faith that you will achieve your goals, no matter what they are.

I'll provide a quick introduction to your mind and how it works. The mind is the control system for the body. I can break it down into three components: your conscious, your subconscious, and your unconscious mind. The conscious is the part of our brain that we're aware of, and it's effectively program number one. When we're conscious, we're aware and choosing our thoughts; we're aware of what we're thinking, and we commonly attribute this to the brain. The truth is that the brain is actually just a stage where the conscious can perform, but for the sake of ease, we will assume they are one for now.

What's important to know is that the mind is an energy field around and out of the body. The brain is the *organ* within the head that harnesses the mind. Now, the brain is designed to protect us—that's its primary function. It will install fear and guide our body based on fear most of the time, because it's trying to protect us.

What's important is to take control of the connection between the brain, the mind, and the body. Because whatever your mind and conscious does, the body will follow. Your mind will always be creating new neurological connections within it which will send different signals down to your body and create different actions.

When we're younger, there's a small part of the brain called the "reticular activator", which is primarily responsible for arousal and motivation. It creates chemicals, hormones, and endorphins that make us happy. What happens is that every time we have an experience, there's a corresponding thought process that follows.

If you had a bad experience as a child with a parent or a bad period of your life where you were in a volatile environment, you likely had anxious thoughts and watched your surroundings. Those anxious thoughts are constantly creating anxiety-inducing chemicals that are sent around the body. Those chemicals make their way through our subconscious mind, through our unconscious mind, and through our body. As it goes through the subconscious and unconscious, it is *writing a program.*

The brain (conscious mind) is program number one, the subconscious mind is program number two, and the unconscious mind is program number three. *We're always running from a program.* These programs are based on conditioning from experiences. The fascinating part is your body writes those programs and you become addicted to the chemical, whether good or bad. If you have a happy childhood, your body gets addicted to the endorphins and dopamine. It craves whatever it's addicted to, so someone who is used to being in a happy environment craves happiness.

Say, for example, there's a young girl who grows up with a dad who beats her mum. She is used to being scared, so her chemicals are fright and vulnerability. Her preprogram is one of a vulnerable person's, and she gets addicted to that chemical. Is there any coincidence that people who grow up in that childhood marry people who beat them? That is the situation that feeds their addiction, and they don't know it. They think they're running their conscious program to make their decisions, but they're not. They're running their subconscious program.

Don't let this worry you—all is not lost. On the contrary, I want you to be excited! You may think, "I've been making all these awful decisions, but now I'm aware and want to do something different!" We can wipe the disk and put in the new program. It's not a problem.

Let's think of a common pre-program—a negative association with money. Many people have a belief system that money is evil, which is ridiculous, and some people have a belief system that money will buy them happiness, which again is ridiculous.

When moving aside from our pre-programming, when it comes to the mind-body connection, we are always creating new connections. These are developed whether we're thinking from our conscious, subconscious, or unconscious mind. It's our choice as to our choices we make. We can choose to make the right connections, and all it takes is a basic understanding of the mind-body connection and how to do that.

When I was harnessing my energy and doing those things, in all honesty, I didn't realise what I was doing at the time. I was creating new connections in my mind through my nervous system, through my spinal cord, and through my legs. I don't know the correct term, but my legs were "dead", if you like.

My thought process at the time was not based on any knowledge, science, or formal background. I just knew that if my body grew from nothing, and if it grew bone tissue, grey matter, and muscle tissue, because everything in our body is a variation of a protein, then there was *hope.* If I've already got my nervous system, my spinal cord, my brain—all these things—why could I not just grow some tissue in my spinal cord? Think about it—if I cut myself, my body grows new tissue because it's hardwired to do this.

Our mind is actually soft-wired. Since it's flexible and malleable, why could I not change the wiring? Why could I not create new connections, rewire that circuit, and regrow a piece of my nerve in my spinal cord? I knew and believed that my body was capable of regenerating that protein, regenerating those cells, and recreating the connections in my spinal cord.

I just needed to learn how to teach my mind to dictate to my body on how to do it.

Everything is connected. Don't ever think it's not. There is a way to fix things, whether they are mentally or physically. Everything is possible. It's just a matter of understanding the process to get there.

When you read my book, I want you to see what I've done and know that it's possible. What I want you to know is that it can all be done because I've done it. *It's all about building belief, and you can latch onto me.*

You're closer to being able to do all those things than you realise. It's just a belief system and a mindset.

Once you master this, you can apply your mind to your life outside your physical goals. Everything you do, you have a preconceived program about it. Many of us have a preprogrammed relationship with money. For example, I believed that being rich would make me greedy or might distort my values. And I never wanted to risk distorting my values or morals. I had to change my belief system with my relationship with money to understand the fact that rich people can be understanding and caring.

For me to get rich, I had to understand that being rich would make me an *even better* person. How? It gave me the financial freedom to write this book. I can now afford to help people. Suddenly, during my subconscious programming, which I'm not aware of (while sleeping or driving, etc.), I am reinforcing the thought that I need money to help people and to be financially free.

Once I embraced this belief system about money for myself, I started to make more positive decisions. I went on a training course for property, which cost one thousand pounds for a four-day training course, and I had told myself I couldn't afford to pay that much. Funny enough, I went out every weekend and spend two to three hundred pounds with my friends drinking. My subconscious was talking myself out of it because it didn't want me to get rich, because it thought this would make me a greedy person.

Once I changed my brain and my way of thinking, I went on the course and learned how to get property deals and investors. Even with no money, I made property deals because I leveraged other peoples' money. I had to get my relationship with money right, and just like the whole walking thing, the whole *everything*, it's always a choice. It's always a belief system. It's always choosing how to harness the energy and how to align your mind-body connection with your belief system.

I want to share with you the day that something incredible happened to outline my success with the mind-body connection.

The physio asked me what my three-week goal was, and this took no thinking about. I replied, "I am going to walk to the physio gym by week three." She looked at me quite bemused, as she clearly did not know how to react to that. She thought I was joking but was too scared to laugh just in case I was not—which I wasn't!

After that, she nervously decided to set my goals for me, which I found quite amusing. Although goal-setting is very important, the most important thing to me at that time was the shift in *belief*. The physio, regardless of how quickly or slowly, had also decided that *walking* was the goal and not wheelchair rehabilitation. This was so exciting to me that the next session could not come fast enough.

When we did finally get into the gym, she pushed me hard, which was an attitude I had longed for and welcomed with open arms. We worked diligently on building strength in my legs. I would be placed on my back with my legs, one at a time, suspended in the air with a sling so that they were weightless. Then I would desperately try to move them. The sweat would pour off me as I would put so much effort into this.

Eventually, I would get a slight movement, causing a swinging action, as if the wind had just blown and caused my leg to swing! It was an amazing feeling to see my leg move on its own accord; I must admit, the feeling was peculiar, because although I had the slightest of movements, I had no control.

At this point, I did not really care. I had achieved more progress! *I had consciously moved my leg!*

I am telling you this to demonstrate that your mind and body can be limited by doing what you've always done, thinking what you've always thought, and staying within your comfort zone. The incredible news is that you can rewrite the programs in your brain, and once you change your thoughts, you'll change your actions, which will effectively change your life.

I harnessed the power of belief, positive thoughts, and energy, and I developed actions that aligned with my goals. I was on the path to walking once more.

## Stop, Take a Moment!

Take a moment to visualise doing something you love. Close your eyes and really submerge yourself in those thoughts. How wonderful do you feel after? It's as if you were actually there doing it. I utilized this technique many times, by daydreaming about walking or angrily fantasizing about running. See how your mind has just changed the way you are feeling, simply through processing some thoughts or memories? Your mind has now affected your body—it is all connected.

As the mind leads, the body will follow.

—*Aaron Timms*

# 6

# THE RELATIONSHIP BETWEEN YOUR SPIRIT AND YOUR CONSCIOUS BRAIN

The spiritual world was thrust upon me in one simple glance, unbeknown to me at the time! Go back with me to that moment in the A & E on the night of my accident. When I was lying there, in a special room by myself, after the commotion had calmed, I just waited. I waited to be airlifted to another hospital, and I was there, strapped down, with painkillers, a mask, and in shock.

As I shared earlier, my dad had entered the room and was quietly sitting with me when I saw something white and I heard a man's voice speaking to me. At the time, I thought it was the doctor, but my dad kept reassuring me that there was no one else in the room.

At the time, I couldn't fathom it out, because I knew what I saw and heard. I thought my dad was just telling me that the doctors weren't there because he was trying to protect me and he didn't want me to hear what they were saying. But I knew what I saw.

When I got to a state of mind when I could read about it, I started studying out-of-body experiences and the connection to the spirit and the soul. I have come to understand that a spirit is part of your conscious mind.

I now know that what I saw and heard was the spirit of my friend, whom I lost in the accident that night. His spirit had left his body, and he had come for one last farewell.

Perhaps it was my own brush with death that enabled me to be so open to this experience. Looking death straight in the eyes gave me a different perspective and a spiritual understanding.

I am sure that to those of you who haven't experienced this, it may sound a bit farfetched. But those of you who have will understand this entirely. This experience helped build a belief for me that there is something more than just this life, this existence.

While at Stoke Mandeville, my mind would constantly switch from thoughts of my injuries to thoughts of loss and grief. I would lie in bed in a trancelike state, not knowing what to feel or think. I tried some cognitive processes, as I try to be a logical thinker generally, and these seemed to work for some time. I would write poems to allow the grief and anger to be released from within me, and I would even choose specific times of the day to grieve and have emotional outbursts. I timed these so I could do this in private and allow myself time away from the grief simply so I could cope. I would use music to manipulate my own feelings. I would listen to sad songs to draw out the pain and fun songs to pick me back up. This probably sounds quite odd to you reading this, but it worked for me at the time, and there is no correct or incorrect way to grieve.

I was in such a desperate state of mind that I was willing to try anything. Grieving for the loss of a loved one is hard, but grieving the loss of two loved ones, particularly so young, as well as the loss of your legs and health all at once, is on *another level.*

Tomorrow's funeral was looming, and I was trembling at the thought of it. Once I had calmed and gathered my thoughts, the solution was quite simple. I made a choice to ask my father to protect me from those fears. All he had to do was respectfully keep people away from me.

The lesson here is if you cannot directly control a situation, or anything, for that matter, then find somebody who can. Do not use this as an excuse. No person can succeed or fail on his own; remember that!

Even when I was supposed to write my cards to put with the flowers, I couldn't cope with this task. Every time I picked up the pen, I broke down. I made a choice to ask my mother to write on my behalf.

Asking for help is often the braver thing to do rather than making mistakes by yourself.

The big day had arrived. As we arrived, there were crowds of people. It was overwhelming in every sense of the word. The fear kicked in again, but I was also delighted to see so many people present in honour of them both. Their mother, whom I was very close to, had asked me to be behind the coffin the whole time; this was an honour and something I felt very strongly about doing. Fortunately, the fear of not doing this was greater than the fear of doing this.

I had prepared a poem while I was alone in my room at Stoke Mandeville, which the vicar read out for me. Words cannot properly describe how I was feeling while this was being read. The pain was immense, it became a physical pain, along with sickness symptoms, probably in the same way I had converted my thoughts into the muscle movement in my legs.

We followed a beautiful horse-drawn funeral carriage as the crowds stood by watching us and sobbing as much as we were. I had a pink rose and a white rose ready for the burial. Even now, when I look back to this moment, knowing what I know, I'm amazed at how the mind can cope with these situations.

I felt strong as I was doing this, the strongest I had felt since the accident. *I know they were with me at that point.*

Again, the situation was what it was, but it was my choice to decide how I viewed this. I chose to take a positive view.

In the days following the funeral, I came down with a serious infection which required urgent surgery. During the surgery, I experienced cardiac arrest, and my heart stopped. All I remember is waking up in intensive care with a sore chest. I was told that I had almost lost my life. I was given several shocks to the chest with a defibrillator, and when this did not work, I was given a shot of adrenaline straight into my heart.

*Another brush with death to remind me how wonderful life is.*

Anyone's belief is their belief—nothing more, nothing less. Nobody really knows, but my beliefs are based on my experiences and my brushes with death, and although I don't fully understand it, I do embrace that there is something more. I believe that we are here for a reason and that we are here to learn lessons and grow. I now believe that the spirit is partly your conscious mind.

As part of my spiritual journey, one of my key lessons was to understand that everyone is equal. I was 21 years old when I had the crash. I was very fit, good at sports, and arrogant—it's just an age thing. Many young men are arrogant. I was then put in a position where I was *genuinely* and *severely* disabled. This experience gave me a next-level understanding about quality of life.

I believe that we come into a body and there is a lesson that we've chosen. When people say that you have a destiny and a pre-emptive script, I personally believe that's rubbish. Most people are preconditioned, yes, but once they become aware and they are conscious, they can rewrite that script and be whomever they want to be and learn whatever they need to learn.

*The spirit is the conscious mind, and the mind is soft-wired. The mind can learn, change, develop and expand, and as it does, so does your soul.*

Little did I know at the time that grief is just another emotion that is easily managed once you have full control over the power of your mind. I will explain this in more detail and give you a full understanding of what is meant by this throughout the book. As you read on, remember that I am simply gathering all my lessons and knowledge for you to discover and use for yourself. You do not need to go through the traumas I have to gather a full understanding. Just be open-minded and be willing to be brave and honest with yourself.

## Stop, Take a Moment!

Think about life, death, and what may come next. Have you ever allowed yourself to fully examine your beliefs? Have you been taught a certain way all your life and failed to question whether that belief truly resonates with you? Are you closed, and do you choose to believe there is nothing more than what we see here on earth?

I want you to harness the power of your beliefs of why you are here and what you are meant to learn. Allow yourself to ask the questions to develop your own belief system.

We are all here to learn.

—*Aaron Timms*

# 7

# HOW YOUR PROGRAM HAS BEEN CREATED

I want you to think back to how you were raised, how you viewed the world, and how, through repetition and conditioning, your program was written. Many of us grow up in a bubble of childhood, following directions and adhering to the seemingly normal thoughts and actions of our parents. It can be years before we question this for ourselves.

Can you think of a time, when as an adult, you handled a situation without any thought? Perhaps you instantly judged someone based on a situation you knew very little about. Or maybe, when confronted with stress, you began to mindlessly do something (for example, eat or clean).

Each experience we have results in a train of thoughts. These thoughts become feelings, and it is the feelings that are stored in our subconscious and unconscious, in the form of memories. Each feeling or memory we store is actually a chemical or hormone, and our body becomes addicted to those chemicals, hormones, and feelings. This is the reason most tend to follow a pattern in their lives. They are addicted to the same way of thinking, addicted to their "familiar self", whether they realise this or not.

It is easy to fall back on our unconscious program, the "familiar self" that we have always relied on, whether it works for us or not. You may have learned some excellent strategies and be addicted to happiness, or you may have learned some passive or aggressive behaviours and be addicted to conflict and drama.

For every person, when they don't want to do something, their preconditioned program in their mind is fear. They're scared of committing to themselves, they are scared to fail, and they talk themselves out of it before it can happen. Again, this is just either the brain working to protect you or your subconscious and unconscious conditioned programs. If you are aware that this is why it's happening, that is the first step to rewriting your automatic program.

There will come a point in your life where you are ready to learn, where you become your higher self, develop, and grow. I want you to understand that preprogramming is deep and that it isn't until you reprogram your thought process that you will truly learn to grow.

When we're not running the conscious program, we are running the subconscious or the unconscious program, both of which are very powerful. Most people are running in this most of the day—probably for 23 hours and 50 minutes of the day. This means that you may be running in your conscious program (not preprogrammed) for only ten minutes of the day. Wow! That means for the remainder of time, you are on autopilot.

The key to breaking free is to download the new software and replace the old. Even your devices require regular updates with new information and tools, so why wouldn't you deserve the same?

The reason that people are so predictable is that they will run the same program all the time and reinforce it. Have you ever heard people say that they're stuck in a rut? They're reinforcing these ways because they are constantly running the same program.

We have 60,000–70,000 thoughts a day, and we're unaware of approximately 65,000 of those thoughts; we don't even know we're having them. Think of it as your computer running applications in the background that constantly reinforce your preconditioned programs. That means that these untrue belief systems that we've installed in ourselves—unknowingly, years ago—are being reinforced 65,000 times a day! And then people wonder why doing an affirmation for five minutes a day for just two weeks doesn't work.

The exciting news is that although you may not understand exactly how it works, you can still program your mind.

Do you use your phone every day? Do you know how it works? How the electricity works? Here's the thing—you don't have to know what it is or how it works to use it every day. It doesn't matter. You might know where it comes from, you might know the processes to create it, but you don't know exactly what electric is. Likewise, just because you don't fully understand the energy within your mind and body, that doesn't mean you can't use it. On the contrary, you use it every day, and it's time to learn to use it to create your desired life.

Quantum physics is much the same. I want you to understand that you don't need to be a quantum scientist to get any of this. You just need to know the process to get this to work and know how to reprogram. All you need to do is follow my steps and what I teach.

**My Top Three Ways to Reprogram**

1. Consciously do something you don't like (or are afraid of) doing, every day. Your body is addicted to the "familiar self", and you must create a new addiction or habit. Keep doing this, and you will create a new habit of success and a new comfort zone that is a productive one. You will naturally grow as a person and achieve things you never thought you could.
2. Maintain a routine. Many people adopt a routine, such as a new eating or training plan, or daily affirmations. The problem is that they plant the seed, and just before it breaks through the surface, they get frustrated from lack of results and quit. They take initial action, and when they don't see what they want after two weeks, they stop. I encourage you to build a routine and *trust the journey.* For me, the days I don't want to do something are the days I do it twice—it's that simple.
3. Remain consistent. Once you develop a new routine, do it every single day without fail. Allow no excuses or doubts to creep in and derail your efforts. It is a true case of mind over matter. A key to maintaining consistency is accountability. For example, I recently decided to sell my car to teach myself a lesson of sacrifice. I realised

> that I had to beat my ego down a bit and drive a rubbish car. I couldn't ask my students or readers to do this without I myself walking the walk. I had three opportunities to sell my car, and I didn't, so I decided to add some accountability. While walking my dog, I did a Facebook Live and said, "Hey, everybody, I didn't sell the car yet, and I promised you I would. I'm going to go home, put it on eBay, and send you the link." I knew damn well that if I didn't do it, I wouldn't have sold the car.

When you are questioning your thoughts, choices, and actions that determine why you fall into the same relationships, why you always handle confrontations in an aggressive manner, and why you aren't allowing yourself to ask your clients for appropriate wages, please understand that your behaviour is the result of the preprogramming of your subconscious and your unconscious mind. As I have said throughout the book, your mind is soft-wired and can easily be reprogrammed by doing new things, stepping out of your comfort zone, building a new routine, and remaining consistent with it.

I distinctly remember lying in the ward speaking with my mother. She said to me, "Do you want anything?"

With no thought at all, I replied, "Yes, a new head and some new legs."

It was a powerful comment, something which was clearly sitting deep within my subconscious mind. Of course, I could not literally change my head and my legs, but I *could indeed completely reprogram my mind* and completely fix the malfunctions in my back and legs. I fully believed this at the time, and I kept going. I kept pushing.

Isn't it time to update and upgrade your software?

Continue reading to learn about how to master the art of daily affirmations (and I mean *daily*), with specific steps to ensure you do them effectively. Through this book, I aim to teach you that anything is possible. Simply change your thoughts, change your actions, and change your life!

## Stop, Take a Moment!

Have you ever said that you were "stuck in your ways"? What are some areas in life where you have seemingly inflexible beliefs? Ask yourself why you feel this way. Was this also the same belief of a parent, a teacher, or someone else who influenced you? Were you taught that there were certain ways to do things and that was it? Have you travelled and met new people and encountered others with different ways of life that also worked? Are you open to expanding your view of the world and what you are capable of?

When you want to be successful as much as you want to breathe, then you will be successful.

*—Aaron Timms*

# 8

# THE POWER OF DELIBERATE PRACTICE

Do you live life aimlessly, bouncing from one moment to the next with no true purpose, focus, or sense of direction? If so, I would like to give you some lessons about deliberate practice.

Deliberate practice is one of many vital ingredients to achieve success in any area of your life. This is a methodical and logical way to perform at a peak level, all the time, without the need to be obsessive or exhausted. Why do some people seem to be exceptional at certain things? Most assume this individual has a *natural gift*, but is that so?

To offer a simple definition, deliberate practice refers to a special type of practice that is purposeful and systematic. While regular practice might include mindless repetitions, deliberate practice requires focused attention and is conducted with the specific goal of improving performance. This is the reason that harnessing the power of your mind, combined with deliberate practice, is so powerful.

When I was at Stoke Mandeville, I first installed true belief in myself and in others around me, and I applied deliberate practice to my recovery.

I must be completely honest with you: I did not know or understand this at the time, but I was applying deliberate practice to my healing and recovery very well. Specifically, I would like to highlight the fact that the brain, when applying deliberate practice with a physical task or movement, will grow new neurons and connections to accommodate the body's newly learnt movement. This is more commonly referred to as "muscle memory".

If you are in a situation like I was and you cannot physically move your limbs, all you must do is close your eyes and imagine movement. The brain will respond in the same way. *As the mind leads, the body will follow!*

While at Stoke Mandeville, my visitors would sit there and stroke my legs while I would intensely imagine the feeling that would create on my skin. Again, this created belief and potential energy, which converted into kinetic energy, which was sent through my nervous system to my nerve endings meeting the skin. It was a great exercise to heal from within and to apply externally.

Again, surrounding yourself with the right people is vital. It is a fact of life that no relationship is neutral—every relationship will either help boost you and add to you or will drag you down or move you backwards.

My powerful physio sessions were followed by a few bad days. I was physically tired and beating myself up, as I seemed to be making no further progress. I was really struggling with the grief, and I felt like the control I had temporarily gained was slipping away. I leaned on a dear friend of mine who was also grieving the loss of my two loved ones. She was wonderfully strong when I was not.

I had momentarily forgotten the key to the success I had found to date. *This was all a choice, conscious or not!*

The medical staff decided to put me on bed rest for a few days, and again, like the time I spent in intensive care, this was a blessing in disguise. I had been so excited about my physio and my legs, I had forgotten that *the true power comes from within your mind.* I had time to gather my thoughts, refocus, and spend more time doing my imagination exercises. I also took the time to plan my physical sessions or workouts, which was truly valuable.

I have read a wonderful and enlightening book called *Peak Performance*, by Anders Ericsson and Robert Pool. Collectively, the authors have studied those "naturally gifted people" for more than thirty years, and their findings are incredible.

The studies on deliberate practice were carried out with a huge variety of experts in their fields, including athletes, musicians, chess players, doctors, salespeople, and many more. The studies included expert research on the physiological, psychological, and neurological anatomy of all the subjects. One common factor discovered in all was that—yes—they do have a special gift, but not what most would be expecting. The special gift is something found in each and every one of us, something we are all born with, and with the *awareness* and correct *application*, we can all use this to give us the "special or natural gift".

We are all born with brains that are flexible and adaptable enough to develop any ability, and this is also true of our bodies. Put simply, the gift of deliberate practice gives us a tremendous amount of control over what our brains can do. In short, the brain responds to triggers by rewiring itself in various ways.

You can be a master of what you choose. There is a myth known as the 10,000-hour rule. Some believe that is the required amount of time to master a skill, but I want you to ignore that.

I'll give you an example. My brother is excellent at golf. Whereas he's played since he was tiny, I had never played in my life. I decided to use deliberate practice and told my brother that I was going to beat him at a round of golf, which he found quite amusing.

I bought a golf set second-hand, then went and hit a hundred balls aimlessly. Not surprisingly, I hit terribly. I then filmed myself hitting five balls, looked at what I did, and took the video to a coach, and he told me what I'd done wrong. After his professional assistance, I hit another five balls and *improved* because of deliberate practice—after just five balls! The key was to talk to a professional, learn the correct procedure, and apply his teachings one by one.

I kept doing this, and within one year, I managed to beat my brother in a round of golf!

To summarize, deliberate practice involves making incremental adjustments by analysing, researching, and fixing, with the addition of finding people to guide you along the way, and then doing it correctly. This can apply to anything in your life that you want to master.

I want you to understand that the healing process comes from within, but you must also apply hard work and deliberate practice to the process.

You need lots of ingredients to make this work. Deliberate practice is something you will come to understand in some depth as you read further.

**My Steps to Incorporate Deliberate Practice**

- You've got to understand where you are when you start. Recognize your starting point.
- Capture what you're doing. I recommend video, and then analyse what's going on.
- Take your evidence or data to a professional and ask him or her to show you how to accomplish this in the proper way.
- Attempt your task again, make small adjustments, review your actions, and take it back to the professional for further assessment.
- Make sure you continually progress rather than remaining stagnant.

With deliberate practice, we're able to see progress so rapidly because we're documenting it. Just this process alone will change you. Although it's easy to live in denial or say, "I'll never do that well", isn't it better to attempt it with deliberate focus so that you can master your skill quickly and effectively?

Although it's naturally hard to be criticised or criticise yourself, know that this uncomfortable feeling results from your brain protecting you from negative emotions, not actual reality. That is the only reason why people are afraid to fail before they even start. They are afraid to stand back and look at their own weakness. I encourage you to be vulnerable, step out of your comfort zone, and focus on growth.

The power of deliberate practice is something that should be recognized in its full glory! When combined with the power of visualization, this is a force so strong you will find it hard to comprehend at the moment. But wait until the results appear, which they will, as long as you commit 100 per cent every day!

It's been said that the subconscious mind cannot distinguish the difference between imagination and reality. Therefore, the objective is to create the "reality" of what we want in our mind and allow our inner world to manifest it into our lives and our bodies.

Deliberate practice has the power to change you. As you now know, this is beyond valuable. You have a rather large advantage over me regarding deliberate practice, because at the time I first started to use it while in rehabilitation, I was not fully aware! But look: you already know this method exists! How will you begin to use deliberate practice to change your life?

## Stop, Take a Moment!

Have you ever done something again and again never to get the hang of it? Perhaps it was while playing a sport, learning a musical instrument, or trying to learn a foreign language? Did you attempt to learn in the same way, again and again, without satisfactorily achieving your goal? Can you imagine what would have happened if you had filmed yourself, went to a sports coach or a music teacher, or immersed yourself in conversation with someone who knew the language? Would you say that your initial efforts were purposeful and focused, or were you afraid to be criticised and fail? Was it easier to say, "I can't do it" than to figure out an efficient way that you could?

Write down three areas of your life to which you could apply deliberate practice, and do it!

________________________________________

________________________________________

________________________________________

________________________________________

________________________________________

________________________________________

________________________________________

*Aaron, you can format these "takeaways" however you would like. In the first two chapters I showed you two ideas.*

I thought I had control of my life and that everything was going well, but the reality was that I was just floating along without really living and creating new opportunities.

—*Aaron Timms*

# 9

# THE IMPORTANCE OF ROUTINE AND CONSISTENCY

If I had decided that I wanted to walk, trained for only a few days, and then quit, do you think I would be walking right now? Absolutely not! I fully committed to a positive belief system and then implemented routine and consistency. It wasn't always easy, but through deliberate and consistent efforts, I am standing here today, supporting my own body weight—something the doctors said I could not achieve.

My daily deliberate practice and imagination exercises were putting me back on track with my physical progress. Regardless of my bad days or how I felt, I was meditating and using my imagination to harness all that kinetic energy through my nervous system and into my legs.

The fruits of my labour were starting to appear more and more every day now. I'll never forget the day that I surprised my mother by lifting my knee approximately two inches off the bed! I'll never forget her reaction; it was as if she held a winning lottery ticket in her hand! This made me feel so powerful and is a memory and feeling I still enjoy reliving to this day.

Now that I had this movement and I saw the true power my mind possessed, I was limitless in my beliefs as to how far my recovery would go. I decided that I needed to stimulate the feeling of standing upright, so I thought that if I could be in an upright position while doing some mind visualization exercises, this would be more powerful and feel more real.

Sure enough, I was correct.

The physio kindly warmed to the idea and helped me get into a standing frame where I could bear my own weight through my legs. I was creating genuine energy that was resonating at the correct frequencies because I was creating a new reality in my mind, deep down, that I was walking. Be under no illusion: I had to put some serious hard physical work into my recovery. The move from the standing frame to the exercise bike was awkward and painful. Being upright was a shock to my system and blood pressure, and the pain was mounting. I had pain in my left leg especially, but I saw this as great. If I could feel pain there, this meant I had stimulated my nerves again and I would feel other sensations there.

As I started to push my legs on the exercise bike, I could feel twinges and odd sensations in my legs, which was awesome. The visualization I had been doing in the standing frame had stimulated my nerves and created those new connections in my brain so fast that my legs were healing further. This gave me a moment of such motivation that I felt as if nothing could stop me.

I started pushing my legs so much, the sweat was pouring off me. The reading on the bike that measures your leg's input, which started at 4 per cent, was going up and up and up! I got this to an astonishing 55 per cent on my left leg and 45 per cent on my right leg! The physio could not believe what she was seeing! She was witnessing a "miracle". I know this is not a miracle but was instead the result of my frame of mind, routine, and consistency.

I was soon rewarded for this state of mind and dedication. My legs were getting stronger, and my momentum was unstoppable. I had decided that I was going to walk into the gym three weeks from the date of my goal-setting meeting with the physio. This day was approaching fast.

I had noticed walking frames in the gym and decided it was my turn to try this. I was told that I was not ready and I would not be given a frame. The physios knew that I would most likely take one anyway, they knew me well enough by now, and I am convinced that they turned a blind eye.

The staff obviously knew I needed to take this leap of faith and had more faith in me than they even realised.

So, guess what I did. I sneaked into the gym in my wheelchair during the lunch hour and found that the gym was closed but not locked. Why was the gym not locked? My answer would be that the universe was offering an *opportunity* and I was *aware* enough to take it.

I grabbed the walking frame and put it in front of my chair, feeling nervous and frightened. Worst case: I would fall and shout for help in a place where lots of professionals were. The reality of most challenges we face is that the worst-case outcome is not *that* bad, but the mind creates a much worse scenario, which is rarely the truth but feels so real so we can hold on to our "familiar self".

With all my strength and determination, I stood up into the walking frame. I tried and nearly fell over. My hands were trembling now, which frustrated me but caused my determination to grow. I repeated this, but this time, I pushed the frame forwards and took a step along with it! I was now starting to cry.

*I had officially taken my first step after being told I would never walk again.* This gave me so much motivation and drive. Again, I pushed the frame forwards and took another step. And again, and again, and again. This was amazing! I felt a bit sick as I had not expected this to be so exhausting. My physical energy was drained, but the energy in my mind was vast, which is the important thing.

Three weeks on from the goal-setting meeting with my physio, I had not walked *to* the gym but instead walked back *from* the gym! I think it is fair to let me have that one. My next goal was set as soon as I landed on my bed: repeat that with crutches instead of the walking frame.

As always, set the next goal immediately. It's very important to always have a goal.

The phone call I made to my mother following this was awesome. I had something solid to give her. I felt good delivering this news, and I believed that my family deserved this—more than I did, in some ways.

Weeks later, I finally got my opportunity to get onto the treadmill with the body-weight support system. This was my time to take literally the next step to walking properly. The excitement of this was overwhelming, but I was met with an odd helpless feeling when I was put into this machine.

This is a situation I want to highlight to you as the reader. I now had a huge decision in this situation—*let* my subconscious control those thoughts and feel helpless or *choose* to take the view that I was walking when I was told I would never walk again. The difference between the two thoughts and the difference between the way I would feel after is vast.

*Remember—it is your choice, and you must choose to take control.*

I could have chosen to quit, to let my stress response and fear kick in, and to stop before I even started, or worse, stop right before the seed I had planted was about to surface. Routine will break that habit of turning on the stress response and begin to provide new programming and results.

We're creatures of habit, and we like routine. We're very predictable as humans. Have you ever woken up in the morning in a good mood—the sun is shining and you feel good—and suddenly, negative thoughts creep in, and suddenly you're in a *mood* just five minutes later? You say, "It's going to be one of those days" and just accept that as fact?

When you run on your old program, your mind and body are in their comfort zone. To break this, routine, consistency, and awareness are all vital. Whether it's your bank balance, marriage, or relationships with friends or family, there is something you must change, because you're clearly not doing something right.

Most of the time, what happens is that people say to me, "I need to change," and so I give them one small exercise to do per day. They'll come back to me a week later and say, "It's not working." When I ask if they did it every day for seven days, they admit that something came up, things got in the way, etc. They couldn't even commit to a five-minute-long activity! It's no surprise it didn't work.

My next suggestion is often "Right. What you need to do is wake up in the morning, have a cold shower to wake you up. Then do your affirmations." On day one, they are pumped, with their energy and state of mind in the right place, but by day four or five, this stops. There is always an excuse. "I was up too late" and "My alarm didn't go off" are common ones I hear.

What causes this is that their subconscious mind is getting out of its comfort zone and works very hard to return to the "familiar self", and they are unaware. As soon as I get a thought of fear or discomfort in my mind, I say out loud, "Thank you for sharing," and then I let it go.

People break their routines because their will is not as strong as their comfort zone. I want you to know that *routine and consistency are paramount.*

You must set yourself a goal. This can be as simple as saying daily affirmations in week one, then switching off the telly and reading for thirty minutes before bed on week two. A small percentage of people take to this quickly, but for most, it will be gradual and will take time. Either way, it's OK.

The moment that consistency gets challenging because you're bored, that's when it's time to up your game, set new goals, and change your routine. Routine and consistency are the most methodical ways to reprogram yourself without having to know everything that I know.

As you have learned from my story, I built a routine of mental exercises and physical exercises, and as I grew, I changed things to continue developing so I would not become stagnant.

Follow routine consistently and stay accountable, and you'll create a new addiction to what you're doing. I'm addicted to learning and self-development. It's been a process, because at first, I wasn't addicted to it, but now I crave the growth and wisdom I achieve.

Retrain your brain to be addicted to what you want and to what serves you.

## Stop, Take a Moment!

Close your eyes and think of three examples in your life where you attempted a new routine but abandoned it shortly after you started. What made you start? What made you quit? Did you write down your goals? Where they measurable so you would know when you had made progress? Did you start off with too many goals at once? Would a gradual progression of development serve you better? Be honest with yourself as to why you abandoned your new habits. Were you afraid to fail? Were you afraid to succeed? Remind yourself that your brain is trying to protect you from feeling negative thoughts—that is all. That the fear you're experiencing is merely an illusion that you can overcome. Do not let your fears become your limits.

---

Make sure that your will is stronger than your comfort zone.

*—Aaron Timms*

---

---

The key to absolute happiness is knowing you have the power to choose what to accept and what to let go.

*—Dodinsky*

---

# 10

# THE LAW OF ATTRACTION

I'd like to share with you a wonderful quote from the book *The Secret*: "Your current reality or your current life is a result of the thoughts you have been thinking. All of that will totally change as you begin to change your thoughts and feelings."

As we know, thoughts become feelings and feelings become actions, so if we are not thinking the correct thoughts (not running the right program), we will not take the right actions towards our goals. The law of attraction always works for us in the way we want it to, when we are conscious and doing our affirmations with an elevated emotion like joy or gratitude. The moment we stop is the moment the universe stops, because the old program starts running again. Once your automatic unconscious program resonates with your desires, the universe will work for you all the time.

After my physical recovery, I was still grieving heavily and decided to travel to Australia to change my environment and continue to heal my mind and spirit. While there, with a dear friend of mine we drove down the East Coast.

Because I was travelling and had some time on my hands, I came across the book *The Secret* and also watched the DVD. I liked the concept, but I didn't fully believe it and needed to see it for myself. I said to my friend Ben, who had no interest in any of this at that time, "I'm going to take this book and give it to a stranger, and I'm going to get it back. I'm going to test the law of attraction. I'm going to test this theory and see what happens."

I got out of the camper van and walked up to a stranger, saying, "There you go, sir. There's a present for you," as I handed him my copy of the book. I immediately put what I had learned into play. I started drawing a picture of the book, thinking about the book, and saying affirmations about the book.

Then I decided I needed to be proactive in trying to get the book.

You can't just do nothing and expect the universe to do all the work. It will mirror the actions you put in. I started visiting local libraries, yet no one had a copy of the book. I even got a small tattoo on my forearm of the emblem from *The Secret* in an effort to attract the book. Needless to say, I was dedicated.

Six weeks later, I started to lose faith.

We travelled to Noosa to visit a friend, who asked, "Hey, boys, my mum's doing a roast on Sunday. Do you fancy popping over? It will be a nice English roast." Since we were still in town and this sounded amazing, we went to his mum's house, and she cooked us a lovely roast dinner. I'm sitting there eating lunch, and my friend's mother asks, "Is that *The Secret* emblem on your arm? Oh, I love the secret!"

I replied, "Oh right, brilliant!"

So, we got in a conversation, and she said, "Lo and behold, I ordered a copy a month ago, and they sent me two. Do you want one? You can go and read it while you're travelling."

I was grinning like the Cheshire cat, and I thought, *Right, this works! Thank you, universe!* After that, I realized that I needed to start putting the law of attraction into place in my life.

My thoughts, actions, drawings, and tattoo all collectively drew the book to me. I had focussed my attention so well that the universe had brought the book to me. I had chosen the correct *vehicles to harness my attention.*

Now that I believed in the law of attraction, Ben got curious as well.

One day, we were talking about our dream wives, and we discussed exactly who she would be, and I decided the law of attraction—the universe—was going to bring her to me. I went onto Google and choose an image. I found an image of a woman who looked like the woman I could see myself marrying. I then put this photo on my phone as the desktop background, and Ben did the same. You know how often you go onto your phone? I saw this image all the time, and put it into my conscious mind, using the law of attraction.

One night, we were in our hostel, and some guys came around asking us to do this pub crawl. We really didn't want to do it and were essentially bullied into it, but once we got there, it turned out to be great. It was a party with fifty women and fifty men. It was a nut-and-bolt party, where all the men were given a bolt, and all women were given a nut, and only one set matched up. We had to walk around meeting people and trying to find the matching pair.

I saw a woman. I approached and talked to her, and—would you believe it—we had a match! We won the prize and talked for the rest of the night. Before going our separate ways for the evening, we exchanged phone numbers.

The next morning, when my alarm went off and I looked at my phone, I said, "Holy shit, Ben! The girl on my phone looks exactly like the girl I met last night—look at her!" Ben and I were both astonished. Naturally, she and I met up again, and I felt a strong connection.

I eventually went home to the UK, and she stayed in Australia for a few more months. Finally, I decided, "Right. I'm going to get her!" The universe had put a huge opportunity in front of me, and I was not going to pass it by. I got on a plane back to Australia, brought her back, and now she is my wife.

It's not just the law of attraction. It's recognizing opportunity. I put it out there. I knew what I was looking for, and when it was presented to me, I was able to recognize the opportunity.

I'm going to go back to touch briefly on the subconscious and unconscious mind, because it's all connected. I want to explain how the energy works, what the energy is, and how the universe pulls us to the energy.

Imagine you have a big pool of energy around you, like a big orange ball. Every time you have a thought, you have a choice as to where you focus that thought. You create a unit of energy that makes an impression, and you are writing a new program.

Energy attracts similar energy. Positive thoughts will attract more positive thoughts and outcomes, and conversely, negative thoughts will attract more negativity. It's just like a magnet.

Magnets attract or they repel, depending on which ends they are, so this energy will resonate at different frequencies depending what that energy is. Once you adjust your focus and energy, you're then putting out an electromagnetic field. You are a magnet, which will attract the same atoms out there in the universe. That's why things come to you despite you not knowing why.

For example, think of the story of the man who was poor and made a lot of money just to lose it again. When poor, he was so focussed on becoming rich that he become rich. When he was rich, he was so focussed on the fear of becoming poor that he lost it again. His thoughts attracted these resulting actions.

An elevated emotion is your ultimate goal. To really be good at using the law of attraction, you must stop wasting energy on the past or future and bring yourself into the now—the present moment, your conscious program.

When you are at that elevated emotion, whatever you are thinking, believing, talking about, and doing, it's all about your ability to recognize opportunities. When you are aware and in a heightened state of mind, you can spot the gifts that life has to offer much more easily.

I was also given another life-changing book at the same time: *Absolute Happiness* by Michael Domeyko Rowland. It explains the law of attraction in a more cognitive and relatable way. When the book came into my hands, I believed that the universe had given me that book.

Many people choose to believe in coincidence. I don't—it's simply an excuse created by your subconscious mind. I believe that everything happens for a reason, and when your electromagnetic field is resonating all the time, at the correct frequency, the law of attraction is working for you, even when you're asleep, in your unconscious program.

Until you make the unconscious conscious it will direct your life, you might call this fate. I call this your subconscious conditioned belief.

## Stop, Take a Moment!

Take a moment to imagine having limitless power to achieve whatever you would like to achieve! When you apply the power of your mind and apply the law of attraction, you are harnessing all the energy in the universe to achieve a specific goal! It is up to you to remain consistent with affirmations, drawings, thoughts, words, and other actions. All the while, the key to recognizing the gifts being delivered to you is awareness.

Think of a goal you'd like to achieve and make it a part of your daily life. Think about it, write about it, speak about it, and ultimately make it so. How powerful!

Wherever you focus your attention, your life will follow.

—*Aaron Timms*

# 11

# THE ART OF AFFIRMATIONS

Affirmations are one of *the most powerful ways* to reprogram the unconscious and subconscious. The reason they do not work for most is that they are not understood fully or are not done for long enough or consistently enough or with true belief.

I will teach you about the power of affirmations and will provide you with an example of the exact method I use every single day.

The unconscious mind is a program that runs every second you are not conscious. Consciousness is being fully aware of your thoughts; it means being able to step outside yourself and view yourself to understand why you are taking those actions and thinking those thoughts. For most of us, we run in this mode for only minutes a day, if at all.

When you're doing affirmations, you're running in the conscious program. Affirmations are so powerful, and when done properly, they are the best tool to start using and winning at the law of attraction.

When you're in a place of consciousness, the place of *the present moment*, you will find that elevated emotion. Your goal could be to find happiness from within, become a millionaire, or achieve the perfect marriage—whatever you desire. When you're in an elevated emotion, you put a clear intention into the universe, and this feels truly wonderful.

What's incredible is that your unconscious and your subconscious cannot define reality or nonreality. They cannot tell the difference between true and false. When you get good at these affirmations, you create an elevated emotion within your mind and body, which is a powerful chemical feeling of the correct type. You then start to emit electromagnetic energy by focusing on the present. It's big and it's powerful, and when you combine it with the right energy and frequency, you become a magnet which will attract the same energy from the universe.

Here is my tested and proven method to properly practice the art of affirmations so that you can be present and mindful and attract what you want from the universe.

**How to Properly Practise Affirmations**

We discussed the necessity of routine and consistency, and for these affirmations to work, you must practice them daily. Every morning, when I wake, this becomes part of my morning routine and helps set the intentions for my day.

An example of one of my affirmations is "I, Aaron Timms, am whole, perfect, strong, powerful, loving, harmonious, and happy." It should be uncomfortable saying what you're saying, because you're reprogramming your mind. I then follow the next steps.

- **Perform a visual affirmation.** While I say the above, I put my thumbs together and follow my thumbs to lock in a visual.
- **Perform an audible affirmation.** Next, I rub my ear lobes so that my ears focus on the words I am saying while I repeat the above.
- **Perform a spiritual affirmation.** To set my affirmation on a spiritual level, I say the above while touching my heart and lowering my tone of voice, because it creates a different frequency.
- **Perform a kinetic affirmation.** Lastly, while saying the above affirmation, I move around. I tap my hands on my knees because it creates an energy.

I do this to create a variety of different energies. Once an energy is created, it can be turned into whatever you want it to be. I do this every day, and on the days I don't want to, I do it three times.

How long does it take for me to reprogram my mind? About two weeks. That's when I see my thoughts and behaviours change, my limitations decrease, and my results increase.

Something that we've already mentioned, but which is worth mentioning again, is that most of us only operate in the conscious program for about ten minutes a day. This is when we are present, aware, and in the now. That means that the primary programs that are running, from the subconscious and unconscious mind, are working in the "old way" for the remainder of the time. It doesn't matter if you are awake or asleep. You are mostly running on these old programs. That's when you go back to resonating with an energy you don't want, and that's when you're undoing all the good work you've done. The law of attraction will almost work against you in these moments, attracting what you always used to attract, so this is where consistency comes in.

Incorporate daily affirmations at the start of each day and generate new energy through visual, audible, spiritual, and kinetic means. After this becomes a consistent routine, ensure that you are open to resulting opportunities, both big and small.

Many believe that a golden gate will appear from the clouds and God will walk out announcing, "Here's the opportunity!" No. The opportunity doesn't appear like that. Yes, it can be large, but often opportunity is small and comes in the form of a friend or a delivery from the postman.

Be fully aware of opportunities resulting from your daily affirmations, and be ready to seize them and reap the benefits! Be open to change once you have manifested it, because your body and brain will keep resisting but your mind is the boss, and you can control this!

## Stop, Take a Moment!

Start your affirmations by selecting two of varying degrees. First, pick an affirmation that's so distant it feels impossible, and then pick one that's easy to get to. Now, go somewhere in the middle, and then use that affirmation every day.

Next, to increase awareness, I want you to write down, every day, one opportunity that is happening that wouldn't have happened before your affirmations. Do you see the difference? Yes or yes?

Learning is not a way of reaching one's potential, but rather a way of creating one's potential.

*—Aaron Timms*

# 12

# CONDITIONING—IDENTIFYING AND CHANGING TRIGGERS

Have you ever thought about those things in your life that trigger a specific response from you? For example, can you think of something that sets you off? How about walking down the street and seeing your ex-partner? Just seeing the face of this individual may incite panic, anger, grief, or nostalgia. In this example, your ex was a trigger, and an obvious one at that.

A trigger is a catalyst that will start a reaction. A catalyst, in scientific terms, is the coming together of two atoms that cause the start of a chemical reaction. A trigger is the catalyst for our way of thinking.

If you have certain triggers in your life that you are unaware of, they will continue to affect you in the same way, every time. We are all guilty of having triggers, and I want to teach you how to identify negative triggers and replace them with positive triggers. When I'm working on myself, I identify a trigger and then work to incorporate it into my routine in a positive way.

Although the "ex" scenario is an example of a blatant trigger, whether you know it or not, you have daily triggers as well. We all do, and they're actually very difficult to identify. I'm going to show you how to change your everyday triggers and reprogram each of those.

I drink far too much coffee, but I love it, and I don't plan on getting rid of it just yet. However, through awareness of my own trigger, I realized that coffee was affecting my mind and my physical processes. I identified that when I was drinking coffee, I felt as if I needed to be busy and proactive. The reason I drank a lot of coffee was that I ran a small engineering company four years ago. I was in that phase of grinding when entrepreneurs are starting out; basically, the wheels were spinning, but they weren't going anywhere. I was running the company, wearing the suit, coming back to meet the customers, running the machines, etc., and my only let-up in a sixteen- to seventeen-hour day was running to the kettle when I had a few minutes. I would drink coffee, regroup, and—bang—I was at it again. Coffee became a trigger for grinding.

Now I have more time to be me. Now, when I'm sitting there on my computer, as I'm doing now, and I've got my coffee, I start off calm and relaxed. But then I drink my coffee, and I became *frantic* in what I am doing. I would flick through emails, change tasks repeatedly, and think, *Whoa—I'm triggering myself to be frantic in my present moment!* I was searching for the "familiar self", and the coffee triggered it. So, I asked, "How do I change that? Because I'm not giving up coffee." Here was my solution.

As I would make my coffee, I'd do my affirmations and incorporate my coffee. I would say aloud, "I am Aaron Timms," do my visual with my thumbs, smell my coffee, and breathe it in. Then I would calmly do my audible and touch my ears, saying, "I am Aaron Timms," and I would smell the coffee and imagine the beans in a very exaggerated manner. I would really taste the flavour, swirl it around in my mouth, and successfully reprogram my mind and body's response to coffee.

So now, when I am sitting in front of my computer or watching the telly, which I rarely do now, I have my coffee and feel empowered. I associate one external force with an internal memory. My inner thoughts and my feelings are now taking my energy from within. I am reconditioning my daily triggers to elevate my emotion.

Your trigger can arrive through any of your senses. The visual of the ex was one example. The smell of food can take you back to childhood, and the sound of a song can transport you to a different emotion.

A lot of people will listen to the same radio station on the way to work because they're running that automatic unconscious program. A habit is simply an automatic unconscious program, but what they don't realize is that radio station is a trigger for an emotion, perhaps stress or anxiety. This is because, at work, their boss always tells them off, so they're triggering anxiety constantly just by having the radio on that station, and they don't even know it.

I have another example to share of how I easily repurposed a trigger in a positive way. I had a business that I set up about two years ago with a partner. Long story short, the business went down the pan, and I lost a lot of money.

Understandably, I was quite bitter and grieving about the process, because I felt like a failure, and I lost money. During this ordeal, I spent a lot of time in my office, and I went into a nearly automatic program for some time without realising it. I lost my awareness and was creating a negative environment in my office. And it's a shame, because I loved my office and spent loads of time there.

A place that I perceived to be my safe place had turned negative, because I spent time grieving in there, thinking, *I should have done this, and he should have done that*, etc. I spent time in my office blaming, and I became resentful of my own office without realizing it.

I had to consciously become aware of what I was doing, and I had to change my office. I got new pictures, I cleared it out, and I started doing my affirmations in there to create positive energy. I successfully changed my environment and trigger, and my office became my safe place, a successful place, once again.

People are very proud and don't always like to admit they're wrong. If they do something to reset, adapt, and change a trigger, it will take time to get reorganized. Changing the way you respond to a trigger is not escapism; it's methodical and is a very heightened way to self-develop and be happy.

As you read this book, you will most likely start identifying triggers, but once you stop reading, it's possible that you'll lose concentration and momentum. This is because your subconscious and unconscious mind will resort to the comfort zone of the preprogram. Your body will go back looking for the "familiar self" and will return to the old programs. Continue with your affirmations to reprogram your software.

Reprogramming a trigger may take some bravery, but it is a brilliant technique and is both absolutely possible and abundantly rewarding. It is life-changing in every sense of the word.

## Stop, Take a Moment!

Identify one trigger per week and devise a way to reprogram it. Perhaps you can listen to a new radio station, drive a new way to work, or, instead of drinking a beer while watching the same evening program, take a walk. Music can do wonders for your mind and can help you reprogram a negative trigger. Identify a song you love that is powerful and pumps you up or uplifts you. Then, while looking at a photo of someone who triggers you or while checking your work email and feeling stressed, listen to the positive song to reprogram your response. Within weeks, you'll have successfully reprogrammed lots of daily triggers.

Remember it is always your choice—take control and responsibility for yourself.

*—Aaron Timms*

# 13

# DEALING WITH ISOLATION

While on your journey to mindfulness, I want you to be aware that your relationships may be affected. This isn't a bad thing, and it's all a part of the process. I want to share why this will happen and what this might look like for you.

When you grow, most people around you will hold on and pull you back, as they are not ready to grow. In short, it is easier for them to pull you down than to pull themselves up.

You must start to build new relationships and be aware of this. You do not need to feel isolated.

This rings home with me. I was in a state of what people call "enlightenment". When I returned from Australia, I was in a heightened state of awareness and elevated emotion. I had read both *The Secret* and *Absolute Happiness* and started putting these principles into play within my life.

Once you become more aware, you will find that your electromagnetic field resonates on a different frequency. I felt truly wonderful, and I wanted to get other people into this state of mind and state of being.

Once you operate on a new frequency, you will start attracting that frequency and stop connecting with the old frequency. For example, say that you've really got some momentum. You go to the pub with your existing friends, and the old conversation doesn't stimulate you anymore. To compound that, they don't want to hear about the law of attraction and think it's rubbish. So here you are, self-developing, and they're not interested because they're not ready.

I felt enlightened but not ready to teach. This is why I believe the universe held me back for a few years. I distinctly remember that I wanted to help all my friends and family, and I thought, *I can teach everybody how to feel this, and help my friends feel this.* Basically, I came back from Australia an annoying person who thought he was a guru. I didn't have *conversations* with people; I *preached* to people.

Although my intentions were in the right place, people began to resent me. I became isolated, and I struggled. I now see the opportunity that I needed, which was to experience isolation, move backwards, and then move forwards again so that I could now teach people how to deal with this. I needed that lesson.

My students need to understand that when they learn from me, they're going to develop so rapidly that they're going to feel isolated. I want my readers to have a little cuddle from me at this point. I want to put my arms around you and say, "It's OK. Isolation is just a belief system, because you're choosing to see those relationships move away and start new ones. If you look in your peripheral field, you'll see the new relationships coming to you. You're not being isolated. You're choosing to see the ending of those relationships."

Isolation is not a fun place to be in, so don't become isolated. It's not just a *deconstruction* period. It's a *rebuilding* period. You are going to rebuild yourself in such a way that you need certain people to come into your life to help you get to the next level. Just know that you'll then go back into your life as a different person.

Back to my story. I thought I was going to have to give up these relationships to move toward my goals. I understand why I thought that at the time, but it's a dangerous place to be in.

If you get a bucket and you put a crab in the bucket, if he's on his own, he'll find a way out. If he's with loads of crabs, every time he tries to get out of the bucket, another crab pulls him down. You will find you feel like your friends and existing relationships are pulling you down because they don't seem to want to move forward with you.

I had a handful of friends that I didn't want to lose, some drinking buddies and some true friends who weren't developing at the same rate I was. I spent hours in tears trying to figure this out. Rather than trying to manipulate the situation, I went to them and told them the truth. I talked about my rapid self-development and of spoke about what I wanted and needed from them. I expected them to turn around with a nervous laugh and push it away, but the ones that I really cared about said, "I really respect what you're doing," and they support me now.

And now I have *new* relationships with the *same* people. Although they are still going about their everyday lives in the same way, they speak to me differently. The relationship, although a little different, is still there. And the relationship grows and thrives and it's wonderful. I can be honest with them and be myself. I can tell them feelings and they respect me, and I respect them. I've learned that I've chosen the belief system of evolving my relationships and instilled a new belief system that doesn't involve isolation.

Nobody can achieve their big goals on their own. No hugely successful person in the world has done it by themselves. The successful ones have had help from their spouses, parents, businesspeople, etc. No one ever fails or succeeds on his or her own.

I want you to know that although isolation is not a fun place to be, you need to be aware of *why* you feel isolated and be aware that you're *not actually isolated.* It's just the feeling of isolation, yet it will feel very real. It's an essential piece to the journey and we need that feeling to learn how to deal with it to then evolve from it.

Keep in mind that it's a good thing. It's just recognizing the opportunity, embracing the change. Although you might be uncomfortable, you will have the opportunity to build new relationships with old friends. As a result, you will become stronger and more honest.

What will happen is you'll think, *Right. I need to speak to them and say this.* By the time you have this planned out, fear sets in, and you talk yourself out of it. I recommend that you use the five-second rule. Count "1, 2, 3, 4, 5," and do it.

For example, say "1, 2, 3, 4, 5", dial the number, and ask, "Can you meet me Wednesday because I need to tell you something that's really important and I need to get it out of my system?" You have set it up, and there's no going back on it. You have made yourself accountable to show up and have the conversation without having to do it immediately.

I want to introduce you to another challenge you may experience while on your path to self-awareness. The battle with your ego is a big one. The ego is an identity that is very difficult to change, and when you start to deal with the isolation, you'll have to change your identity. You've got your ego, the true self, and the false self.

The best way to deal with ego is to become your true self. If the ego doesn't have an identity, it can't exist.

When you go through a period of self-development and your ego suffers, you then must learn to be your *true* self. Only when you become that self in *all* environments will you deal with your ego.

Most people have a set of egos. I think that we can identify with having multiple personalities, depending on our environments. Suppose that in front of your friends, you're the "cool guy", but in front of your mum, you are her polite, well-behaved son. When you bring them all together at once, your mum and your friends, your ego doesn't know how to act. When you become your true self, you win the battle against your ego because you don't have so many selves at once.

I can be emotional, and I can be honest about my feelings because I am *not* worried about what people think, because I'm being *me*. I am my true self, and I can tell my story to everyone because I'm the same in all situations.

If you are out of sync, you will never have your true self intact. The false self is someone we've built up and is conditioned by our environment, our past relationships, and our experiences, and it's effectively the subconscious mind. It's a confused self. When we learn to be in our true self, to be in the energy we want, the old ego starts to disappear.

I want you to know that there is more energy spent living in your false self than if you were living in your true self. Your ego needs to be built and constantly reinforce the false self. Don't spend the energy faking it. Spend the energy making it, in your true form, your true self.

When you do those ten minutes of your affirmations, when you become your true self, you'll live as that self every day, even while asleep. In the morning, you'll feel brilliant because your unconscious is running your true program. You're in a wonderful cycle of feeling and being awesome. Isn't that what you want?

## Stop, Take a Moment!

Are you living as your one true self? Are you faking it? In which environments are you faking it and why? What identities do you relate to? Are you a different person depending on which group you are in? Why and when do you change? Are you afraid of your family, friends, or co-worker's seeing your true self? Are you ready to be you?

Relationships are never neutral, they either push you up or pull you down.

*—Aaron Timms*

# 14

# BALANCE—HOW YOU DO ANYTHING IS HOW YOU DO EVERYTHING

It's fact that in everything you need balance. Relationships, careers, businesses, your feelings, your thoughts—everything requires balance, and this balance needs to come from within.

Most people find something that resonates during self-development, and then they go and throw it all at one facet of their life. If you take everything we've talked about concerning elevated emotion, energy, and the law of attraction and throw it at one area, that is OK, but only for a short while. Why? If you throw it all at your career, how is your marriage going to fare? And if your marriage starts to suffer, then the way you feel about yourself and your mood will start to suffer, which will negatively affect your career. What will happen is—imagine this—each aspect of your life then suffers and, to put it bluntly, becomes unhappy. This is precisely why balance is essential.

Do you know the reason I'm successful right now? Because I'm balancing my business life and my finances, I actively spend time with my wife on our marriage (not just time together), I spend quality time with my friends, and I'm in the *now*.

When you're in each aspect of your life, it's important you are present. Here's an example of how deep and meaningful being present can be. Recently I spent a morning with my father in my office at home. We turned off our phones and all distractions and talked. Both of us were fully in the moment and nowhere else. The conversation we had, and that time we spent together, has literally created a much deeper and more beautiful relationship between us. Something that will impact our lives forever. Our relationship is now well balanced.

Balance is so important, and I think it's vital that you understand that. When I ran the engineering company, I bought that company from my friend's grandfather. My intention was that I would buy it and my friend would run it, and I would act as a silent partner.

Instead, I did that "typical busy entrepreneur" thing, and before I knew it, I was absorbed. I made the company *reliant on me*, which is the worst thing an entrepreneur could do. The company tripled its turnover, and the profit margin grew. As they say, any idiot can create turnover; not everyone can create profit.

I had so much attention on the business, I wasn't seeing my wife enough. I'd ask if she would stop at the shop so that we could have a mini picnic lunch in my office. And this wasn't during the week, mind you; this was on a Saturday and Sunday. So, I was spending time with my wife in my office while working. No! That was so out of balance! Not surprisingly, my marriage was suffering as a result.

I also remember having so much work on a Saturday evening that rather than going to the pub and having a beer and a meal with my friends, I would invite them to spend time with me at my work. I'd ask, "How about you help me out a bit Saturday night? I'll give you some money and we can have a few beers. I'll lock the doors so no one knows what we're doing." Because they were my friends, they did it!

Suddenly, the whole balance was gone. My friends didn't like doing it, but because of our established relationships, like the one I had with my wife, everyone went along with it, but it wouldn't have lasted for long. There was such a lack of balance that my life was about to *implode*.

I learned my lesson, I became aware, and I sold the company before it imploded. Because the company relied on me so much, I recognized that as soon as I imploded—which I would have done sooner or later—my wife would have left me, my friends would have made other friends, and my family would have gotten sick of me never seeing them. At the time, I thought that missing family meals was OK because I was working and that it was justifiable, but no, it is not.

The one thing in my life that was successful, would have been *unsuccessful* in a short period.

After that, someone approached me and asked that I invest in his company. I agreed and said, "I want half the company, but want you to run it and do it all for me." I decided that the company needed to be so distanced from me that I didn't need to know what was going on and didn't need to be there. This was the *other* ultimate one-eighty that entrepreneurs do.

This was the other worst possible move I could have made as an entrepreneur.

This didn't work out. I lost a lot of money, became depressed and resentful, and let my marriage be negatively affected. Thankfully, I had the awareness to realize this and spent a lot of time with my wife and fixed it. To this day, we have days that we switch the phone off and spend time together.

My property company is run from a place of balance now. I spend time on it, and I also put it down. When I am focussed on my business, I am not focused on anything else, but when I'm not focussed on my business, I don't focus on it at all. It must be balanced.

It's the same with my marriage. When I'm focused on my business, my wife leaves me alone, or—because she helps me run my business—we don't engage and both work on separate elements together, in the same room, but we remain focussed. Even our marriage has balance within the business.

As I close this chapter, having illustrated the need for balance and what it looks like when things are off, I want to remind you to schedule time for yourself. This is not selfish, and the moment you work on yourself and get yourself right, the more valuable you'll be to the people around you.

This all goes back to my initial relationship with money. Now that I have reprogrammed my mind, I ask, "Am I *greedy* because I have a healthy passive income, or am I *giving* because I can spend the time creating this book, teaching workshops to genuinely help people?"

Just know, I didn't get to this position to help others without a lot of work on myself. I encourage you to make the investment in your best self as well.

## Stop, Take a Moment!

Get a seven-day schedule, divide each day into twenty-four hours, and then, for one week, write what you are doing. Just write one word in each box, and do not miss one box. The key to this exercise is honesty. If you feel a bit embarrassed, then you are unbalanced now. Analyse your results and start scheduling in time for family, business, friends, and personal development. Follow this new schedule for a week and see what happens! Be brave and honest! Be ready to create new habits of success and happiness.

Balance must come from within.

*—Aaron Timms*

# 15

# VALUES—FINDING YOUR WHY

To become who you want to be, you need to find your why. If you don't know your why, you don't know your end goal, and it's impossible to plan your journey.

I will help you diagnose your own why. Many people stop at the first level without going deeper, and I believe that if you don't know your why, you either aren't asking enough questions or aren't asking the right questions.

If you ask most people what their motivation is, they will say that it is money. But I believe this is rarely the case, and they all have deeper whys that they have not yet discovered. I'd like to show you an example of the process:

Q: Why are you working so many hours? A: Because I need more money.

Q: Why do you need more money? A: Because I want to provide a better life.

Q: Why do you want a better life? A: Because I want to be happy.

Q: Why do you want to be happy and what will make you happy? A: My wife.

Q: How does your wife relate to your happiness? A: With more money, I can buy her things, which will make us both feel happy.

As you see, it wasn't about the money. It was about showing love to someone you cared about to make *them* happy. Of course, when someone you love is happy, it makes you feel good, plain and simple.

I've been chasing the coin for the last four years. I've been trying to get rich, and I have been successful with it, off and on. I went away on a weekend to learn to retrain my mind on the triggers and associations with money. I knew the reason I had a glitch in my business was that I had negative associations with money and I hadn't fully identified my why. Now I know that my why isn't related to money at all! Instead, it's teaching and helping people. Now that my why is in the right place, I know my goals and am self-motivated.

*You can't plan your journey if you don't know your destination.*

Think of it as a trip. Once you know your destination, you develop a timeline and an itinerary, plan which flight to take, etc. By knowing my destination, my why, and my goal, I make the journey properly, and I successfully reach my destination.

You need to align your values with your goals and your dreams. Most people will tell you their values are great because most people are good people. But even good people have incoherent values. To my friend who comes to me and asks, "OK, you've got a great marriage. How do you do it?" I say that it's because my values are right and my routine is right. I aligned my new routine with my values.

For example, I once told someone who wanted a better marriage, "Go back home, and when your wife gets up for work in the morning, you're going to surprise her. Set your alarm thirty minutes before she wakes up, iron her clothes for work, make her a cup a tea, and when she wakes, give her the tea and tell her that you've ironed her clothes. Do that for a week and see what happens."

He went away a bit confused and said, "OK" with *that* face, as if it was the hardest job in the world. And when he came back to me, he said, "I just can't. The way I was brought up, men don't iron clothes. It's not what we do. I want a good marriage, but that's not for me."

I said, "OK, that's interesting. Are your values lining up with your goals? Do you value feeding your ego more than you value your wife's happiness? Are you telling me that your values are in line with your dreams? Because they're not. Go and get your values right, make a routine, and then see how your marriage is."

*The primary obstacle to growth is the ego.*

I'll give an example of how my values line up with my goals and demonstrate to you why my marriage is so happy and why people come to me for advice.

My wife was heavily pregnant with our first. We took our dog for a walk, and my wife became tired. I knew that she needed to sit down, so I asked myself what I could do.

We were very close to a woods where there was a massive training camp for the army. I created a solution, and I said, "OK, stop." I could get on my hands and knees and create a bench so she could sit down for a bit. I thought, *What if these army guys, doing drills, see me like a dog with my wife sitting on me?* I almost didn't do it because my preprograming almost stopped me, and my ego almost won.

I asked myself "do you care more about your wife's health or what a stranger thinks of you Aaron"? It's obvious I care *more* about my wife's health and happiness than what strangers think about me. I put my values in line and the decision was easy. It's not just doing that one act but doing it repeatedly in a relationship. The act of doing it changes your routine, your marital routine, and, in turn, your partner's routine. You can argue that it's *manipulation for the greater good*, but you've now become addicted to a happy environment and a happy marriage. It then becomes easy—you don't need to force yourself to make your wife a cup of tea because you just make her one.

This applies to careers, money, anything. Once it becomes a subconscious addiction and routine, it becomes simple. The actual reason is that you've found a purpose, and you have started by understanding your why.

I'd like to tell you about a point in my life when my values were unclear. This is a good example of when people think they have good values, but they don't, because values and morals are slightly different.

When I was younger, before my accident, I got in trouble a lot. During my late teens and early twenties, I would get arrested all the time for doing silly things like getting into fights. But my morals were good, and I never harmed anyone. I've always been a caring person, and I never stole from anyone.

I'm a good example of a person with good morals but bad values. I valued my ego far more than I valued my education at points. I was more interested in going out on a Friday night and doing what the cool kids did. I could have done better in my grades.

There's a quote about good intentions: "Everybody always does their best at that time." Sometimes people do awful things, but it's because they have the wrong knowledge, wrong values, and wrong morals.

You need to evaluate your values constantly. When you achieve true enlightenment and you have perfect balance, your values are in check, you have the perfect marriage, a good relationship with your children or parents, and you have a passive income, you are set.

I encourage you to work on your values all the time.

Your values are never going to stay the same, and they may go up and go down, so there is merit to re-evaluating your values. The more you know your true self, the better your values will align with your goals.

Mine aren't perfect yet, because if they were, I'd be exactly where I want to be right now. My life is pretty damn good, but I haven't changed enough lives—yet!

I want to help people to heal. The joy I experience from doing that my why, so I value getting up early. Do I get up early enough? Do I value sleep over helping people? Are these values in line? Is there balance? These are examples of questions I regularly ask myself to ensure that my values balance out and always line up with my why, my purpose.

You're always developing, and you should always be striving for the perfect balance. Life is fluid. The fluidity of life is going to change your values. Make sure your value is totally in sync with your why. It's a constant state of evolution and of growth to be constantly in sync with your values. This is a good thing. *You're evolving not battling.*

As I wrap up my book, I hope that I have inspired you, given you someone to believe in, and provided some strategies you can apply today to fulfil your higher purpose.

A quotation I would like to briefly discuss is as follows: “What the eye of man can see and believe, he can achieve.” Such a wonderful quotation.

Your mind has the power to see any image that you want it to see. You have a choice to choose what you see, and you also have a choice as to what you truly believe that you can achieve. There are no excuses; the boundaries are your *choice*. It is also your choice to have *no* boundaries.

Remember—I healed myself with 0 per cent chance.

In this instance, I am directly referring to the healing process, but this is true of any goals you may have. This is also true of the business and income that you would like to build and create. This is also true of the relationships that you would like to build in your life, and the list goes on. Again, the power of your mind is the most powerful force in the universe but only when it is being used to its *full potential*.

It’s in me. It’s in you. Thank you for letting me help you find it. Just like in my story, it was all about *taking that first step* toward your new life. Now, it’s your turn, and I believe in you.

## Stop, Take a Moment!

Before reading this book, would you have imagined that someone in my shoes could have ever walked again—especially knowing the severity of my injuries and the opinions of the medical community?

Has my book helped you build belief, changed what you thought about your own goals and possibilities? What are you excited about? What are you inspired to do? What steps are you going to take today?

From now on, you can leave behind the ways of the many, t join the path of the few.

—*Aaron Timms*

Thank you for reading my book!

I very much hope that this book has added value to your life. May I ask you a quick favour? If this book has added value to your life, if you feel like you're better off after reading it and you see that *Belief-Bound Mind* can be a new beginning for you, I'm hoping you'll do something for someone you love:

*Give this book to them.* Let them borrow your copy. Ask them to read it. Or better yet, get them their own copy, maybe as a simple gesture of friendship.

Or it could be for no special occasion at all, other than to say, "Hey, I love and appreciate you, and I want to help you live your best life. Read this." Sometimes a book is all a person needs to get back on track and start to believe that greatness is possible.

If you believe, as I do, that being a great friend or family member is about helping your friends and loved ones to become the best versions of themselves, I encourage you to share this book with them.

*Belief-Bound Mind* is how I was able to live my dream life. It's time for others to live theirs, too.

—Aaron Timms

www.facebook.com/AaronTimmsOfficial/
www.instagram.com/aaron_timms_official/

The next step:

To continue your journey, please visit my website, where you will be offered support and guidance by me personally. Enter your email in the box provided on the home page, and I will be in touch.

*https://www.aarontimmsofficial.com/*

Printed in the United States
By Bookmasters